My family is special

Anna
Rayo

Mónica
Armiño

First edition: April 2021

© Author: Anna Rayo, 2021
© Illustrations: Mónica Armiño, 2021
© Editorial el Pirata, 2021
c. Ribot i Serra, 162 bis, 08208, Sabadell
info@editorialelpirata.com
www.editorialelpirata.com

International Rights © Tormenta, 2019
rights@tormentalibros.com | www.tormentalibros.com
Translation by Emma Garner for BigTranslation

ISBN: 978-84-17210-99-1
Legal deposit: B 4488-2021
Printed in the EU

MIX
Paper from
responsible sources
FSC® C018236

For Paloma,
who will never fully believe
that she finally has a book
dedicated to her.
Thank you for
your unconditional support.

And for Luis and Mael,
my little family.

NEXT WEEK IT'S
MY BIRTHDAY.

I HAVE INVITED MY WHOLE FAMILY
TO CELEBRATE IT!!

THERE ARE FAMILIES
WITH A DAD AND A MOM.

THERE ARE ALSO FAMILIES
WITH A DAD, A MOM, AUNTS, UNCLES,
LOTS OF COUSINS...
AND EVEN A PET!

SOME FAMILIES ONLY HAVE
A DAD OR A MOM.
BUT THEY GIVE SO MUCH LOVE
THAT IT IS AS IF THERE WERE TWO OF THEM.

SOMETIMES, TWO FAMILIES
JOIN TOGETHER IN ONE.
THERE WILL NEVER BE A DULL MOMENT!

THERE ARE ALSO FAMILIES
WITH TWO MOMS OR TWO DADS.
LIKE EVERYBODY ELSE,
THEY LOVE TO GIVE KISSES AND CUDDLES!

SOMETIMES,
A FAMILY LIVES SEPARATELY.
THE CHILDREN HAVE TWO HOUSES
IN WHICH THEY ARE LOVED.

THERE ARE FAMILIES
WITHOUT CHILDREN
WHO HAVE EXTRA LOVE
FOR THEIR NIECES AND NEPHEWS!

SOME CHILDREN
DON'T LOOK LIKE THEIR FAMILY
ON THE OUTSIDE,
BUT ON THE INSIDE
THEY ARE EXACTLY THE SAME.

OTHERS LIVE ALONE.
BUT WHEN WE RECEIVE A VISIT...
WE HAVE THE BIGGEST
FAMILY OF ALL!

DID YOU NOTICE
THAT WITH EACH FAMILY
THERE WAS A LETTER
AND A PIECE OF PAPER
FOLDED IN DIFFERENT WAYS?

SEE IF YOU CAN FIND THEM ALL!